A PVERPORA SALVE·

T GRATIA SACRI

In Praise of Our Lady

The Madonna and Child. *Raphael*

In Praise of
Our Lady

Edited by Elizabeth Jennings

With a Foreword by Cardinal Hume

B. T. BATSFORD LTD. LONDON

ISBN 0 7134 4087 2

Typeset by Keyspools Ltd, Golborne, Lancs
and printed in Great Britain by
The Pitman Press Ltd
Bath, Avon
for the publishers
B. T. Batsford Ltd.
4 Fitzhardinge Street
London W1H 0AH

Contents

Foreword

This selection of poems about Our Lady has been culled from the work of many poets, from the earliest days of the Christian era to our own day. Their poems enshrine the fruits of their contemplation of her whom Wordsworth acclaimed as 'our tainted nature's solitary boast'. They speak eloquently of Mary's virtues, of her person, of her mothering of the Son of God, and of her mothering of us.

I hope that all who use this book will find in it springs to true devotion, to true praise of Our Lady, which has its origin in faith, and both comes from the Father and leads back to Him.

BASIL HUME. *Archbishop of Westminster*

The Illustrations

The endpapers are reproduced from a twelfth-century mosaic of the Annunciation, in the apse of Sta Maria in Trastevere, Rome *(The Mansell Collection, London)*. The reproductions of medieval stained glass come from *Swiss Stained Glass of the Fourteenth Century* (Batsford, 1949) and *Stained Glass ... from French Cathedrals* (Batsford, n.d.)

Acknowledgments

The editor and publishers would like to thank the following for permission to reproduce certain copyright poems:
G. K. Chesterton, *A Christmas Carol* from COLLECTED POEMS. Reprinted by permission of Methuen & Co Ltd., London.
Dante, *Canto XXXIII* from DIVINE COMEDY (translated by Geoffrey Bickersteth). Reprinted by permission of Basil Blackwell (Publisher).
T. S. Eliot, extract from *The Dry Salvages* from FOUR QUARTETS. Reprinted by pemission of Faber and Faber Ltd.
Thom Gunn, *Jesus and His Mother* from THE SENSE OF MOVEMENT. Reprinted by permission of Faber and Faber.
Geoffrey Hill, *Ave Regina Coelorum* from TENEBRAE (1978). Reprinted by permission of Andre Deutsch.
David Jones, extract from *The Tutelar of the Place* from THE SLEEPING LORD. Reprinted by permission of Faber and Faber Ltd.
Robert Lowell, *Our Lady of Walsingham* from POEMS 1938–1939. Reprinted by permission of Faber and Faber Ltd.
Edwin Muir, *The Annunciation* from THE COLLECTED POEMS OF EDWIN MUIR. Reprinted by permission of Faber and Faber Ltd.
Norman Nicholson, *Carol* from FIVE RIVERS. Reprinted by permission of Faber and Faber Ltd.
Rainer Maria Rilke *Of the Marriage at Cana, Visitation of the Virgin, Rest on the Flight to Egypt* from MARIEN⁄LEBEN (translated by Stephen Spender). Reprinted by pemission of Stephen Spender.
R. S. Thomas, *Pietà* from PIETA. Reprinted by permission of Granada Publishing Ltd.
Karol Wojtyla, *Her Amazement at Her Only Child* and *John Beseeches Her* from EASTER VIGIL (translated by Jerzy Peterkiewicz). Reprinted by permission of Hutchinson Publishing Group.
W. B. Yeats, *The Mother of God* from COLLECTED POEMS. Reprinted by permission of M. B. Yeats, Anne Yeats and Macmillan London Ltd.

Introduction

To put together a collection of poems 'In Praise of Our Lady' has been an exceptionally difficult task. There are numerous poems, prayers and hymns about her in the very early periods of English literature, and there are also many which were written right up to the Reformation. After that, the veneration of Our Lady was not permitted and only Catholic poets wrote such poems. Unfortunately many of the good and even great poets such as Vaughan and Herbert were not Catholics. However, Donne, rather surprisingly, *did* write one or two poems about the Blessed Virgin. So, even more astonishingly, did Wordsworth and Byron.

It is when we come to the twentieth century that poets turned to this subject again, but unless they were practising Catholics or Anglicans they tended to treat Our Lady as a subject just as they would write about any other subject: that is, with objectivity rather than as a personal invocation.

The obvious exception to this is, of course, Gerard Manley Hopkins who, though a nineteenth-century poet, was not published until 1918, only four years before *The Waste Land*. His *May Magnificent* and *The Blessed Virgin Compared to the Air We Breathe* are poems of a very high order. They communicate Hopkins' passionate devotion to Our Lady and they are also marvellously sustained poems in which form and content are inseparable. Rilke wrote a whole sequence about Our Lady which is more an imaginative re-creation of her life than a hymn of eloquent praise.

It has been hard to chose poems from the mediaeval period because there are so many on this subject, but I have attempted to include some of the best. The poems are arranged chronologically in that a poem about Our Lady's birth is placed before the Annunciation and Nativity but, in the case of carols or poems of praise, I have placed these here and there among poems limited to a temporal event. It has been a delight to be able to include in translation two poems by Pope John Paul II* who is a fine poet as well as a linguist, athlete, diplomat and a holy man whom the whole world has come to love.

ELIZABETH JENNINGS

* Karol Wojtyla

The Death of the Virgin. *Thirteenth-century stained glass*

A Maiden Peerless

A Maid peerless
    Hath borne God's son.
Nature gave place,
When ghostly grace
    Subdued reason.

As for beauty,
Or high gentry,
    She is the flower
By God elect
For this effect,
    Man to succour.

Of virgins queen,
    Lodestar of light,
Whom to honour
We ought endeavour
    Us day and night.

ANONYMOUS

As I Lay On A Night

As I lay up on a night
   My thought was on a berd so bright
That men clepen Marye full of might,
    Redemptoris mater.

To here cam Gabriel with light,
And seid 'Heil be thou, blissful wight,
To ben clepèd now art thou dight
    Redemptoris mater.'

At that wurd that lady bright
Anon conseived God full of might.
Than men wist weel that sche hight
    Redemptoris mater.

Whan Jhesu on the rode was pight,
Mary was doolful of that sight,
Til sche sey him rise up right,
    Redemptoris mater.

Jhesu, that sittest in hevenè light,
Graunt us to comen beforn thy sight,
With that berd that is so bright,
    Redemptoris mater.

ANONYMOUS

The Virgin and Child. *Thirteenth-century stained glass*

The Virgin and Child in the Stable. *Bernardo Daddi*

Carol

Mary laid her Child among
    The bracken-fronds of night—
And by the glimmer round His head
    All the barn was lit.

Mary held her Child above
    The miry, frozen farm—
And by the fire within His limbs
    The resting roots were warm.

Mary hid her Child between
    Hillocks of hard sand—
By singing water in His veins
    Grass sprang from the ground.

Mary nursed her Child beside
    The gardens of a grave—
And by the death within His bones
    The dead became alive.

NORMAN NICHOLSON (1914–   )

Mary Speaks

From: Paradise Regain'd I

These growing thoughts my Mother soon perceiving
By words at times cast forth inly rejoyc'd,
And said to me apart, high are thy thoughts
O Son, but nourish them and let them soar
To what highth sacred vertue and true worth
Can raise them, though above example high;
By matchless Deeds express thy matchless Sire.
For know, thou art no Son of mortal man,
Though men esteem thee low of Parentage,
Thy Father is the Eternal King, who rules
All Heaven and Earth, Angels and Sons of men,
A messenger from God fore-told thy birth
Conceiv'd in me a Virgin, he fore-told
Thou shouldst be great and sit on *David's* Throne,
And of thy Kingdom there should be no end.
At thy nativity a glorious Quire
Of Angels in the fields of *Bethlehem* sung
To Shepherds watching at their folds by night,
And told them the Messiah now was born,
Where they might see him, and to thee they came;
Directed to the Manger where thou lais't,
For in the Inn was left no better room:
A Star, not seen before in Heaven appearing
Guided the Wise Men thither from the East,
To honour thee with Incense, Myrrh, and Gold,
By whose bright course led on they found the place,
Affirming it thy Star new grav'n in Heaven,
By which they knew thee king of *Israel* born.

JOHN MILTON (1608–1674)

The Conception of Our Ladie

Our second Eve putts on her mortall shrowde,
  Earth breedes a heaven for God's new dwelling-
    place;
Nowe ryseth upp Elias' little cloude,
  That growing shall distill the shoure of grace;
Her being now begins, who, ere she ende,
Shall bringe the good that shall our evill amende.

Both Grace and nature did their force unite
  To make this babe the summ of all their best;
Our most, her lest, our million, but her mite,
  She was at easyest rate worth all the reste:
What Grace to men or angells God did part,
Was all united in this infant's hart.

Fower onely wightes bredd without fault are nam'd,
  And all the rest conceivèd were in synne;
Without both man and wife was Adam fram'd,
  Of man, but not of wife, did Eve beginne;
Wife without touch of man Christ's mother was,
Of man and wife this babe was bredd in grace.

ROBERT SOUTHWELL (1560–1595)

Mary's Girlhood

(*For a Picture*)

This is that blessed Mary, pre-elect
   God's Virgin. Gone is a great while, and she
   Dwelt young in Nazareth of Galilee.
Unto God's will she brought devout respect,
Profound simplicity of intellect,
   And supreme patience. From her mother's knee
   Faithful and hopeful; wise in charity;
Strong in grave peace; in pity circumspect.

So held she through her girlhood; as it were
   An angel-watered lily, that near God
    Grows and is quiet. Till, one dawn at home,
She woke in her white bed, and had no fear
   At all,—yet wept till sunshine, and felt awed:
    Because the fulness of the time was come.

DANTE GABRIEL ROSSETTI (1828–1882)

Head of the Virgin. *From a fifteenth-century wall painting*

I Will Have No Other Spouse

Vpon a lady my loue ys lente,
With owtene change of any chere,
That ys louely & contynent
And most at my desyre.

Thys lady ys yn my herte pyght;
Her to loue y haue gret haste.
With all my power & my myght,
To her y make myne herte stedfast.

Therfor wyll y non othur spowse,
Ner none othur loues, for to take;
But only to here y make my vowes,
And all othur to forsake.

Thys lady ys gentyll & meke,
Moder she ys & well of all;
She ys neuur for to seke,
Nothur to grete ner to small.

Redy she ys nyght & day,
To man & wommon & chylde ynfere,
Gyf that they awght to here say,
Our prayeres mekely for to here.

To serue thys lady we all be bownde,
Both nyght & day yn euery place,
Where euur we be, yn felde or towne,
Or elles yn any othur place.

Pray we to thys lady bryght,
In the worshyp of the trinite,
To brynge vs alle to heuen lyght—
Amen, say we, for charyte.

ANONYMOUS

Our Ladie's Nativitye

Joye in the risinge of our orient starr,
That shall bringe forth the Sunne that lent her light;
Joy in the peace that shall conclude our warr,
And soone rebate the edge of Saton's spight;
Load/starr of all engolfd in worldly waves,
The card and compasse that from shipwracke saves.

The patriark and prophettes were the floures
Which Tyme by course of ages did distill,
And culld into this little cloude the shoures
Whose gracious droppes the world with joy shall fill;
Whose moysture suppleth every soule with grace,
And bringeth life to Adam's dyinge race.

For God, on Earth, she is the royall throne,
The chosen cloth to make His mortall weede;
The quarry to cutt out our Corner/stone,
Soyle full of fruite, yet free from mortall seede;
For heavenly floure she is the Jesse rodd
The childe of man, the parent of a God.

ROBERT SOUTHWELL (1560–1595)

Our Ladye's Spousalls

Wife did she live, yet virgin did she die,
   Untowchd of man, yet mother of a sonne;
To save herself and childe from fatall lye,
   To end the webb whereof the thredd was spoone,
In mariage knottes to Josephe she was tyde,
Unwonted workes with wonted veyles to hide.

God lent His paradice to Josephe's care.
   Wherein He was to plante the tree of life;
His Sonne, of Joseph's childe the title bare,
   Just cause to make the mother Josephe's wife.
O blessèd man! betrothd to such a spouse,
More blessd to live with such a childe in house!

Noe carnall love this sacred league procurde,
   All vayne delites were farre from their assent;
Though both in wedlock bands them selves assurde,
   Yet strait by vow thy seald their chast entent:
Thus had she virgins', wives', and widowes' crowne,
And by chast childbirth doubled her renowne.

ROBERT SOUTHWELL (1560–1595)

The Madonna in Majesty. *Duccio di Boninsegna*

I Saw a Sight

This enders night
  I saw a sight
    All in my sleep;
Mary, that may,
She sang 'Lullay'
    And sore did weep.

To keep she sought
Full fast about
    Her son fro cold.
Joseph said 'Wife,
My joy, my life,
    Say what ye wold.'

'No thing, my spouse,
Is in this house
    Unto my pay;
My son, a king
That made all thing,
    Lieth in hay.'

'My mother dear,
Amend your cheer,
    And now be still;
Thus for to lie
It is soothly
    My Father's will.

'Derision,
Great passion,
    Infinitely,
As it is found,
Many a wound
    Suffer shall I.

'On Calvary
That is so high
    There shall I be,
Man to restore,
Nailèd full sore
    Upon a tree.'

ANONYMOUS

The Virgin and Child. *From a fifteenth-century woodcut*

Of Alle Kinges King

I saw a fair maiden
    Sitten and singe,
Sche lullėd a litel child,
    A swetė lording.

That echė lord is that
    That made allė thinge;
Of allė lordės he is lord,
    Of allė kingės king.

There was mekel melody
    At that childės berthe;
Allė tho wern in hevenė bliss
    They made mekel merthe.

Aungele bright they song that night,
    And seiden to that child,
'Blessėd be thou, and so be sche
    That is bothe meke and mild.'

Prey we now to that child,
    And to his moder dere,
Graunt hem his blessing
    That now maken chere.

ANONYMOUS

The Mother of God

The threefold terror of love; a fallen flare
Through the hollow of an ear;
Wings beating about the room;
The terror of all terrors that I bore
The Heavens in my womb.

Had I not found content among the shows
Every common woman knows,
Chimney corner, garden walk,
Or rocky cistern where we tread the clothes
And gather all the talk?

What is this flesh I purchased with my pains,
This fallen star my milk sustains,
This love that makes my heart's blood stop
Or strikes a sudden chill into my bones
And bids my hair stand up?

W. B. YEATS (1865–1939)

The Virgin

From Ecclesiastical Sonnets, 1821

Mother, whose virgin bosom was uncrost
With the least shade of thought to sin allied;
Woman, above all women glorified,
Out tainted nature's solitary boast;
Purer than foam on central ocean tost;
Brighter than eastern skies at daybreak strewn
With fancied roses, than the unblemished moon
Before her wane begins on heaven's blue coast;
Thy image falls to earth.
                Yet some, I ween,
Not unforgiven the suppliant knee might bend
As to a visible power, in which did blend
All that was mixed and reconciled in thee
Of mother's love with maiden purity,
Of high with low celestial with terrene.

WILLIAM WORDSWORTH (1770–1850)

To Our Blessed Lady

In that, O Queen of queens, thy birth was free
   From guilt, which others doth of grace bereave,
   When in their mother's womb they life receive,
God as his sole-born daughter loved thee.
To match thee like thy birth's nobility,
   He thee his Spirit for thy spouse did leave,
   Of whom thou didst his only Son conceive,
And so wast linked to all the Trinity.
Cease then, O queens, who earthly crowns do wear,
   To glory in the pomp of worldly things!
If men such high respect unto you bear,
   Which daughters, wives and mothers are of kings,
      What honour should unto that Queen be done,
      Who had your God for father, spouse and son?

HENRY CONSTABLE (1562–1613)

Ave Regina Coelorum

There is a land called Lost
at peace inside our heads.
The moon, full on the frost,
vivifies these stone heads.

Moods of the verb 'to stare',
split selfhoods, conjugate
ice-facets from the air,
the light glazing the light.

Look at us, Queen of Heaven!
Our solitudes drift by
your solitudes, the seven
dead stars in your sky.

GEOFFREY HILL (1931–   )

The Annunciation

The angel and the girl are met.
Earth was the only meeting place.
For the embodied never yet
Travelled beyond the shore of space.
The eternal spirits in freedom go.

See, they have come together, see,
While the destroying minutes flow,
Each reflects the other's face
Till heaven in hers and earth in his
Shine steady there. He's come to her
From far beyond the farthest star,
Feathered through time. Immediacy
Of strangest strangeness is the bliss
That from their limbs all movement takes.
Yet the increasing rapture brings
So great a wonder that it makes
Each feather tremble on his wings.

Outside the window footsteps fall
Into the ordinary day
And with the sun along the wall
Pursue their unreturning way.
Sound's perpetual roundabout
Rolls its numbered octaves out
And hoarsely grinds its battered tune.

But through the endless afternoon
These neither speak nor movement make,
But stare into their deepening trance
As if their gaze would never break.

EDWIN MUIR (1887–1959)

The Annunciation. *Konrad Witz*

The Madonna and Child. *Lorenzo Monaco*

My Soul Doth Magnify The Lord

And Mary said: My soul doth
magnify the Lord:
And my spirit hath rejoiced in God
my Saviour.
Because he hath regarded the
humility of his handmaid: for behold
from henceforth all generations shall
call me blessed.
Because he that is mighty hath done
great things to me: and holy is his
name.
And his mercy is from generation
unto generation, to them that fear
him.
He hath shewed might in his arm:
he hath scattered the proud in the
conceit of their heart.
He hath put down the mighty from
their seat, and hath exalted the
humble.
He hath filled the hungry with
good things: and the rich he hath sent
empty away.
He hath received Israel his servant,
being mindful of his mercy.
As he spoke to our fathers: to
Abraham and to his seed for ever.

ST LUKE, Chapter 1, vs. 46–55

Annunciation

From: La Corona

Salvation to all that will is nigh;
That All, which alwayes is All every where,
Which cannot sinne, and yet all sinnes must beare,
Which cannot die, yet cannot chuse but die,
Loe, faithfull Virgin, yeelds himselfe to lye
In prison, in thy wombe; and though he there
Can take no sinne, nor thou give, yet he'will weare
Taken from thence, flesh, which deaths force may trie.
Ere by the spheares time was created, thou
Wast in his minde, who is thy Sonne, and Brother;
Whom thou conceiv'st, conceiv'd; yea thou art now
Thy Makers maker, and thy Fathers mother;
Thou'hast light in darke; and shutst in little roome,
Immensity cloysterd in thy deare wombe.

JOHN DONNE (1578–1631)

Head of the Virgin. *Piero della Francesca*

The Birth of Jesus. *From a fifteenth-century MS*

Our Blessed Lady's Lullaby

Upon my lap my Sovereign sits,
    And sucks upon my breast;
Meanwhile His love sustains my life
    And gives my body rest.
      Sing lullaby, my little boy,
      Sing lullaby, my livés joy.

When Thou hast taken Thy repast,
    Repose, my babe, on me.
So may Thy mother and Thy nurse,
    Thy cradle also be.
      Sing lullaby, my little boy,
      Sing lullaby, my livés joy.

I grieve that duty doth not work
    All that my wishing would,
Because I would not be to Thee
    But in the best I should.
      Sing lullaby, my little boy,
      Sing lullaby, my livés joy.

Yet as I am and as I may,
    I must and will be Thine,
Though all too little for Thyself.
    Vouchsafing to be mine.
      Sing lullaby, my little boy,
      Sing lullaby, my livés joy.

My wits, my words, my deeds, my thoughts,
    And else what is in me,
I rather will not wish to use,
    If not in serving Thee.
        Sing lullaby, my little boy,
        Sing lullaby, my livés joy.

My babe, my bliss, my child, my choice,
    My fruit, my flower and bud,
My Jesus, and my only joy,
    The sum of all my good.
        Sing lullaby, my little boy,
        Sing lullaby, my livés joy.

My sweetest, and the sweetest most
    That heaven could earth deliver,
Soul of my love, spirit of my life,
    Abide with me for ever.
        Sing lullaby, my little boy,
        Sing lullaby, my livés joy.

Live still with me, and be my love,
    And death will me refrain,
Unless Thou let me die with Thee,
    To live with Thee again.
        Sing lullaby, my little boy,
        Sing lullaby, my livés joy.

RICHARD ROWLANDS (1565–1620)

Virgin and child. *Twelfth-century stained glass*

Tell Me, Swete Son, I Thee Praye

'Mary moder, I am thy child,
  Thogh I be laid in stall;
Lordès and dukes shall worsship me
  And so shall kingès all.
Ye shall well see that kingès three
  shall come the twelfthè day.
For this behest yeve me thy brest,
  And sing, By by, lullay.'

'Now tell me, swete son, I thee pray,
  Thou art me leve and dere,
How shuld I kepe thee to thy pay
  And make thee glad of chere?
For all thy will I wold fullfill,
  Thou weteste full well in fay;
And for all this I will thee kiss,
  And sing, By by, lullay.'

The Birth of Christ. *Hans Baldung*

'My dere moder, whan time it be,
    Thou take me up on loft,
And settè me upon thy knee,
    And handell me full soft;
And in thy arme thou will me warme,
    And kepè night and day;
If that I wepe, and may not slepe,
    Thou sing, By by, lullay.'

'Now swetè son, sin it is so,
    That all thing is at thy will,
I pray thee grauntè me a bone,
    If it be both right and skill,
That child or man that will or can
    Be mery upon my day,
To blisse hem bring, and I shall sing
    Lullay, By by, lullay.'

ANONYMOUS

Her Amazement at Her Only Child

Light piercing, gradually, everyday events;
a woman's eyes, hands
used to them since childhood.
Then brightness flared, too huge for simple days,
and hands clasped when the words lost their space.

In that little town, my son, where they knew us together,
you called me mother; but no one had eyes to see
the astounding events as they took place day by day.
Your life became the life of the poor
in your wish to be with them through the work of your hands.

I knew: the light that lingered in ordinary things,
like a spark sheltered under the skin of our days –
the light was you;
it did not come from me.

And I had more of you in that luminous silence
than I had of you as the fruit of my body, my blood.

KAROL WOJTYLA (1920–   ) (*Translated by Jerzy Peterkiewicz*)

Once in Royal David's City

Once in royal David's city
  Stood a lowly cattle shed,
Where a Mother laid her Baby
  In a manger for his bed:
Mary was that Mother mild,
Jesus Christ her little Child.

He came down to earth from heaven,
  Who is God and Lord of all,
And his shelter was a stable,
  And his cradle was a stall;
With the poor, and mean, and lowly,
Lived on earth our Saviour holy.

And through all his wondrous childhood
  He would honour and obey,
Love, and watch the lowly Maiden,
  In whose gentle arms he lay;
Christian children all must be
Mild, obedient, good as he.

For he is our childhood's pattern,
    Day by day like us he grew,
He was little, weak, and helpless,
    Tears and smiles like us he knew;
And he feeleth for our sadness,
And he shareth in our gladness.

And our eyes at last shall see him,
    Through his own redeeming love,
For that Child so dear and gentle
    Is our Lord in heaven above;
And he leads his children on
To the place where he is gone.

Not in that poor lowly stable,
    With the oxen standing by,
We shall see him; but in heaven,
    Set at God's right hand on high;
When like stars his children crowned
All in white shall wait around.

MRS C. F. ALEXANDER (1828–1895)

Mary with the Animals. *Albrecht Dürer*

Visitation of the Virgin

She still walked easily in the beginning.
Yet already was sometimes aware when climbing
of her marvellous body's life within.
And then, pausing for breath, she stood upon

the high hills of Judea. But spread wide
around her, was her fullness, not the land.
Walking, she felt: no one would overstride
the greatness which she now could understand.

And the need pressed on her now to lay her hand
on the other body, which had gone on further.
And the women leaned to one another, and
they touched each other on the dress and hair.

Each one filled with her own sacred good
used the other as shield in her plight.
Ah, the saviour in her still was bud,
but in her cousin's womb, the Baptist could,
and did, leap in rapture of delight.

RAINER MARIA RILKE
(*Translated by Stephen Spender*, 1909–   )

The Virgin's Cradle-Hymn

Sleep, sweet Babe, my cares beguiling;
Mother sits beside thee smiling;
   Sleep, my Darling, tenderly.
If thou sleep not, Mother mourneth,
Singing as her wheel she turneth;
   Come, soft slumber, balmily.

SAMUEL T. COLERIDGE (1772–1834)

Nativitie

From: La Corona

Immensity cloysterd in thy deare wombe,
Now leaves his welbelov'd imprisonment,
There he hath made himselfe to his intent
Weake enough, now into our world to come;
But Oh, for thee, for him, hath th'Inne no roome?
Yet lay him in this stall, and from the Orient,
Starres, and wisemen will travell to prevent
Th'effect of *Herods* jealous generall doome.
Seest thou, my Soule, with thy faiths eyes, how he
Which fils all place, yet none holds him, doth lye?
Was not his pity towards thee wondrous high,
That would have need to be pittied by thee?
Kisse him, and with him into Egypt goe,
With his kinde mother, who partakes thy woe.

JOHN DONNE (1578–1631)

The Child Than Spak in His Talking

This lovely lady sat and song,
    And to her child con say,
'My sone, my broder, my fader dere,
    Why liest thou thus in hay?
My swete brid, thus it is betid,
    Thogh thou be king veray;
But nevertheles I will not cese
    To sing, By by, lullay.'

The child than spak in his talking,
    And to his moder said,
'I bekid am for heven king,
    In cribbe thogh I be laid;
For aungeiles bright done to me light.
    Thou knowest it is no nay.
And of that sight thou mayst be light
    To sing, By by, lullay.'

'Now swete sone, sin thou art king,
    Why art thou laid in stall?
Why ne thou ordende thy bedding
    In sum gret kinges hall?
Me thinketh it is right, that king or knight
    Shuld lie in good aray;
And than among it were no wrong
    To sing, By by, lullay.'

ANONYMOUS

Our Lady and all the Angels, Pray for Me

I Pray thee, lady, the moder of crist,
  Praieth youre sone me for to spare,
With al angels and Iohn Baptist,
  And al youre company that now ys thare,
  Al holichurch, for my welfare.
    Graunt me of youre merites a participacion,
    And praieth oure lorde for my saluacyon.

ANONYMOUS

Overleaf: The Birth of the Virgin. *Gioseppi Salviati*

I Sing of a Maiden

I sing of a maiden
   That is makeless:
King of all kingès
   To her son she ches.

He came all so stille
   There his mother was,
As dew in Aprille
   That falleth on the grass.

He came all so stille
   To his mother's bower,
As dew in Aprille
   That falleth on the flower.

He came all so stille
   There his mother lay,
As dew in Aprille
   That falleth on the spray.

Mother and maiden
   Was never none but she;
Well may such a lady
   Goddès mother be.

ANONYMOUS

Nun's Well, Brigham

The cattle crowding round this beverage clear
To slake their thirst, with reckless hoofs have trod
The encircling turf into a barren clod;
Through which the waters creep, then disappear,
Born to be lost in Derwent flowing near;
Yet o'er the brink, and round the lime⁄stone cell
Of the pure spring (they call it the 'Nun's Well,'
Name that first struck by chance my startled ear)
A tender spirit broods—the pensive shade
Of ritual honours to this fountain paid
By hooded votaresses with saintly cheer;
Albeit, oft the Virgin⁄Mother mild
Looked down with pity upon eyes beguiled
Into the shedding of 'too soft a tear.'

WILLIAM WORDSWORTH (1770–1850)

The 'Ave' Hour

'Ave, Maria'; o'er the earth and sea,
That heavenliest hour of heaven is worthiest thee.

'Ave, Maria'; blessed be the hour,
    The time, the clime, the spot, where I so oft
Have felt a moment in its fullest power
    Sink o'er the earth so beautiful and soft,
While swung the deep bell in the distant tower,
    Or the faint dying day-hymn stole aloft,
And not a breath crept through the rosy air,
And yet, the forest leaves seemed stirred with prayer.

'Ave, Maria'; 'tis the hour of prayer;
    'Ave, Maria'; 'tis the hour of love;
Ave, Maria'; may our spirits dare
    Look up to thine and to thy Son's above;
'Ave, Maria'; oh, that face so fair;
    Those down-cast eyes beneath the Almighty Dove—
What though 'tis but a pictured image strike,
That painting is no idol—'tis too like.

LORD BYRON (1788–1824)

The Annunciation: the Virgin. *Fra Angelico*

...riritatis nobilis ...erietur un...

GVRAM PRETEREVNDO CAVE NE SILEATVR AVE

Jesus and His Mother

My only son, more God's than mine,
Stay in this garden ripe with pears.
The yielding of their substance wears
A modest and contented shine:
And when they weep with age, not brine
But lazy syrup are their tears.
'I am my own and not my own.'

He seemed much like another man,
That silent foreigner who trod
Outside my door with lily rod:
How could I know what I began
Meeting the eyes more furious than
The eyes of Joseph, those of God?
I was my own and not my own.

And who are these twelve labouring men?
I do not understand your words:
I taught you speech, we named the birds,
You marked their big migrations then
Like any child. So turn again
To silence from the place of crowds.
'I am my own and not my own.'

Mary in the Stable. *Fourteenth-century stained glass*

Why are you sullen when I speak?
Here are your tools, the saw and knife
And hammer on your bench. Your life
Is measured here in week and week
Planed as the furniture you make,
And I will teach you like a wife
To be my own and all my own.

Who like an arrogant wind blown
Where he may please, needs no content?
Yet I remember how you went
To speak with scholars in furred gown.
I hear an outcry in the town;
Who carried that dark instrument?
'One all his own and not his own.'

Treading the green and nimble sward
I stare at a strange shadow thrown.
Are you the boy I bore alone,
No doctor near to cut the cord?
I cannot reach to call you Lord,
Answer me as my only son.
'I am my own and not my own.'

THOM GUNN (1929–   )

66

To Our Blessed Lady

Sovereigne of Queenes: If vayne Ambition move
   my hart to seeke an earthly prynces grace:
   shewe me thy sonne in his imperiall place,
   whose servants reigne, our kynges & queenes above.
And if alluryng passions I doe prove,
   by pleasyng sighes: shewe me thy lovely face:
whose beames the Angells beuty do deface:
and even inflame the Seraphins with love.
So by Ambition I shall humble bee:
   when in the presence of the highest kynge
   I serve all his, that he may honour mee.
And love, my hart to chaste desyres shall brynge,
   when fayrest Queene lookes on me from her throne
   and jealous byddes me love but her alone.

Sweete Queene: although thy beuty rayse upp mee
   from syght of baser beutyes here belowe:
   yett lett me not rest there: but higher goe
   to hym, who tooke hys shape from God & thee.
And if thy forme in hym more fayre I see,
   what pleasure from his diety shall flowe,
   by whose fayre beames his beuty shineth so
   when I shall yt beholde æternally.
Then shall my love of pleasure have his fyll,
   when beuty self in whom all pleasure ys,
   shall my enamored sowle embrace & kysse:
And shall newe loves, & newe delyghtes distyll,
   which from my sowle shall gushe into my hart
   and through my body flowe to every part.

HENRY CONSTABLE (1562–1613)

Of the Marriage at Cana

Could she be anything but very proud
of him who made the plainest things become
lovely? And was not the high, large-accustomed
night as though beside itself when he appeared?

Did not his having lost himself once, also
add unbelievably to his renown?
And did the wisest not change mouths into
ears, to hear him? Had not the house grown

new, at his voice? Ah, surely in those days
she had restrained herself a hundred times
from beaming forth with her delight in him.
And so she followed after him, amazed.

But there on that day at the wedding feast
when, unexpectedly, more wine was needed,
she looked, and begged a gesture at the least
and did not understand when he protested.

Then he did it. And she saw much later
how she had thrust him then upon his way.
Now he'd become a real miracle-maker,
and in this act unalterably there lay

the sacrifice. Yes, written and decreed.
Then on that day, was it prepared already?
She; it was she had driven on the deed
in the blindness of her vanity.

At table, heaped with vegetables and fruits,
she shared the joy, and never understood
that the water from her own tear-ducts,
with this wine, had been transformed to blood.

RAINER MARIA RILKE
  (*Translated by Stephen Spender*, 1909—)

Rest on the Flight into Egypt

These ones who but recently had flown
from amid the massacre of children:
oh how imperceptibly they'd grown
slowly greater through their wandering.

Scarcely had their timid looking backward
shed the worst extremities of fear
than they themselves, upon their gray mules, had
already brought whole cities into danger.

For when they, so small in the great region,
—a nothing almost—came near the strong temples,
all the idols there began to topple
seemed as if betrayed, and lost their reason.

Is it thinkable that when they passed
everything fell in such desperate rages?
And they came to fear themselves at last.
The child alone was namelessly at ease.

Nonetheless, they had to sit and ponder
on acount of this. But just then ... see:
the silent, overhanging, shady tree,
like one serving them, bent over:

bowed to them. And this tree was the same
wreaths of which bind and protect the brows,
everlastingly, of the dead pharaohs,
bowed down. Felt within itself that now
new crowns bloomed. They sat as in a dream.

RAINER MARIA RILKE
(Translated by Stephen Spender, 1909–)

The Flight into Egypt. *Giotto*

O What avails me ...

From: Paradise Regain'd II

O what avails me now that honour high
To have conceiv'd of God, or that salute
Hale highly favour'd, among women blest;
While I to sorrows am no less advanc't,
And fears as eminent, above the lot
Of other women, by the birth I bore,
In such a season born when scarce a Shed
Could be obtain'd to shelter him or me
From the bleak air; a Stable was our warmth,
A Manger his, yet soon enforc't to flye
Thence into *Egypt*, till the Murd'rous King
Were dead, who sought his life, and missing fill'd
With Infant blood the streets of *Bethlehem;*
From *Egypt* home return'd, in *Nazareth*
Hath been our dwelling many years, his life
Private, unactive, calm, contemplative,
Little suspicious to any King; but now
Full grown to Man, acknowledg'd, as I hear,

By *John* the Baptist, and in publick shown,
Son own'd from Heaven by his Father's voice;
I look't for some great change; to Honour? no,
But trouble, as old *Simeon* plain fore-told,
That to the fall and rising he should be
Of many in *Israel*, and to a sign
Spoken against, that through my very Soul
A sword shall pierce, this is my favour'd lot,
My Exaltation to Afflictions high;
Afflicted I may be, it seems, and blest;
I will not argue that, nor will repine.
But where delays he now? some great intent
Conceals him: when twelve years he scarce had seen,
I lost him, but so found, as well I saw
He could not lose himself; but went about
His Father's business; what he meant I mus'd,
Since understand; much more his absence now
Thus long to some great purpose he obscures.
But I to wait with patience am inur'd;
My heart hath been a store-house long of things
And sayings laid up, portending strange events.

JOHN MILTON (1608–1674)

The Adoration of the Magi. *Albrecht Dürer*

Mother of Particular Perfections

Queen of the differentiated sites, administratix of the
demarcations, let our cry come unto you.
                              In all times of imperium save us when
the *mercatores* come to save us
                    from the guile of the *negotiatores* save us from the *missi*,
from the agents
                    who think no shame
by inquest to audit what is shameful to tell
                                        deliver us.
When they check their capitularies in their curias
                              confuse their reckonings.
When they narrowly assess the *trefydd*
                        by hide and rod
                        by *pentan* and pent
by impost and fee on beast-head
                        and roof-tree
and number the souls of men
                        notch their tallies false
disorder what they have collated.
When they proscribe the diverse uses and impose the
rootless uniformities, pray for us.
                        When they sit in *Consilium*
to liquidate the holy diversities
                        mother of particular perfections
                        queen of otherness
                        mistress of asymmetry

patroness of things counter, parti, pied, several
protectress of things known and handled
help of things familiar and small
                 wardress of the secret crevices
                 of things wrapped and hidden
mediatrix of all the deposits
                    margravine of the troia
empress of the labyrinth
                 receive our prayers.
When they escheat to the Ram
                      in the Ram's curia
the seisin where the naiad sings
           above where the forked rod bends
or where the dark outcrop
         tells on the hidden seam
pray for the green valley.
When they come with writs of oyer and terminer
                 to hear the false and
                 determine the evil
according to the advices of the Ram's magnates who serve
the Ram's wife, who write in the Ram's book of Death.
In the bland megalopolitan light
      where no shadow is by day or by night
be our shadow.

DAVID JONES (1895–1974)

The Blessed Virgin Compared to the Air We Breathe

Wild air, world-mothering air,
Nestling me everywhere,
That each eyelash or hair
Girdles; goes home betwixt
The fleeciest, frailest-fixed
Snowflake; that's fairly mixed
With, riddles, and is rife
In every least thing's life;
This needful, never spent,
And nursing element;
My more than meat and drink,
My meal at every wink;
This air, which, by life's law,
My lung must draw and draw
Now but to breathe its praise,
Minds me in many ways
Of her who not only
Gave God's infinity
Dwindled to infancy
Welcome in womb and breast,
Birth, milk, and all the rest
But mothers each new grace
That does now reach our race –
Mary Immaculate,
Merely a woman, yet
Whose presence, power is
Great as no goddess's
Was deemèd, dreamèd; who
This one work has to do –
Let all God's glory through,
God's glory which would go
Through her and from her flow
Off, and no way but so.

I say that we are wound
With mercy round and round
As if with air: the same
Is Mary, more by name.
She, wild web, wondrous robe,
Mantles the guilty globe,
Since God has let dispense
Her prayers his providence:
Nay, more than almoner,
The sweet alms' self is her
And men are meant to share
Her life as life does air.
    If I have understood,
She holds high motherhood
Towards all our ghostly good
And plays in grace her part
About man's beating heart,
Laying, like air's fine flood,
The deathdance in his blood;
Yet no part but what will
Be Christ our Saviour still.
Of her flesh he took flesh:
He does take fresh and fresh,
Though much the mystery how,
Not flesh but spirit now
And makes, O marvellous!
New Nazareths in us,
Where she shall yet conceive
Him, morning, noon, and eve;
New Bethlems, and he born
There, evening, noon, and morn —
Bethlem or Nazareth,
Men here may draw like breath
More Christ and baffle death;
Who, born so, comes to be
New self and nobler me
In each one and each one
More makes, when all is done,
Both God's and Mary's Son.

Again, look overhead,
How air is azurèd:
O how! nay do but stand
Where you can lift your hand
Skywards: rich, rich it laps
Round the four fingergaps.
Yet such a sapphire⁄shot,
Charged, steepèd sky will not
Stain light. Yea, mark you this:
It does no prejudice.
The glass⁄blue days are those
When every colour glows,
Each shape and shadow shows.
Blue be it: this blue heaven
The seven or seven times seven
Hued sunbeam will transmit
Perfect, not alter it.
Or if there does some soft,
On things aloof, aloft,
Bloom breathe, that one breath more
Earth is the fairer for.
Whereas did air not make
This bath of blue and slake
His fire, the sun would shake,
A blear and blinding ball
With blackness bound, and all
The thick stars round him roll
Flashing like flecks or coal,
Quartz⁄fret, or sparks of salt,
In grimy vasty vault.

So God was god of old:
A mother came to mould
Those limbs like ours which are
What must make our daystar
Much dearer to mankind;
Whose glory bare would blind
Or less would win man's mind.
Through her we may see him
Made sweeter, not made dim,
And her hand leaves his light
Sifted to suit our sight.
    Be thou then, O thou dear
Mother, my atmosphere;
My happier world, wherein
To wend and meet no sin;
Above me, round me lie
Fronting my forward eye
With sweet and scarless sky;
Stir in my ears, speak there
Of God's love, O live air,
Of patience, penance, prayer:
World-mothering air, air wild,
Wound with thee, in thee isled,
Fold home, fast fold thy child.

GERARD MANLEY HOPKINS (1876–1889)

Invocacio Ad Mariam

From: The Second Nun's Prologue

And thow that flour of virgines art alle
Of whom that Bernard list so wel to write,
To thee at my bigynnyng first calle;
Thou confort of us wrecches, do me endite
Thy maydens deeth, that wan thurgh hire merite
The eterneel lyf, and of the feend victorie,
As man may after reden in hire storie.

Thow Mayde and Mooder, doghter of thy Sone,
Thow welle of mercy, synful soules cure,
In whom that God for bountee chees to wone,
Thow humble, and heigh over every creature,
Thow nobledest so ferforth oure nature,
That no desdeyn the Makere hadde of kynde
His Sone in blood and flessh to clothe and wynde.

Withinne the cloistre blisful of thy sydis
Took mannes shap the eterneel live and pees,
That of the tryne compas lord and gyde is,
Whom erthe and see and hevene, out of relees,
Ay heryen; and thou, Virgine wemmelees,
Baar of thy body—and dweltest mayden pure—
The Creatour of every creature.

Assembled is in thee magnificence
With mercy, goodnesse, and with swich pitee
That thou, that art the sonne of excellence,
Nat oonly helpest hem that preyen thee,
But often tyme, of thy benygnytee,
Ful frely, er that men thyn help biseche,
Thou goost biforn, and art hir lyves leche.

Now help, thow meeke and blisful faire mayde,
Me, flemed wrecche, in this desert of galle;
Thynk on the womman Cananee, that sayde
That whelpes eten somme of the crommes alle
That from hir lordes table been yfalle;
And though that I, unworthy sone of Eve,
By synful, yet accepte my bileve.

And, for that feith is deed withouten werkis,
So for to werken yif me wit and space,
That I be quit fro thennes that most derk is!
O thou, that art so fair and ful of grace,
Be myn advocat in that heighe place
Theras withouten ende is songe 'Osanne,'
Thow Cristes mooder, doghter deere of Anne!

And of thy light my soule in prison lighte,
That troubled is by the contagioun
Of my body, and also by the wighte
Of erthely lust and fals affeccioun;
O havene of refut, o salvacioun
Of hem that been in sorwe and in distresse,
Now help, for to my werk I wol me dresse.

GEOFFREY CHAUCER (?1340–1400)

A Christmas Carol

The Christ-child lay on Mary's lap,
    His hair was like a light.
(O weary, weary were the world,
    But here is all aright.)

The Christ-child lay on Mary's breast,
    His hair was like a star.
(O stern and cunning are the kings,
    But here the true hearts are.)

The Christ-child lay on Mary's heart,
    His hair was like a fire.
(O weary, weary is the world,
    But here the world's desire.)

The Christ-child stood at Mary's knee,
    His hair was like a crown,
And all the flowers looked up at Him,
    And all the stars looked down.

G. K. CHESTERTON (1874–1936)

Madonna and Child. *Ferrarese School*

St Bernard's Prayer To Our Lady

From: Dante's Paradiso: Canto XXXIII

O Virgin-Mother, Daughter of thy Son,
O creatures all the lowliest, loftiest One,
Term of God's counsel, fixed ere time begun.
Our human race thou hast to such degree
Ennobled in thy Maker's eye, that he
His Creature's Child hath not disdained to be.
Kindled anew within thy womb's pure shrine,
Did burn the love beneath those glow benign
Bloomed in eternal peace this Flower divine.
Here, unto us, thou art the noonday Light
Of Charity—below, in earth's dark night,
Thou art of Hope the living Fountain bright.
Lady, so great thou art, thy power so high,
Who longs for grace, nor breathes to thee his sigh,
Would have his wishes without wings to fly.
Thy bounty succoureth not him alone
Who asks for it; but, oftentimes is known
Freely to come ere the demand hath flown.
In thee all mercy, clemency we find;
In thee all splendour—all in thee combined,
Whatever is of good in human kind.
O Queen, who canst whate'er thou wilt, I pray
That he who hath such wonders seen to-day,
'Neath thy protection ever safe may stay.

Translated by Geoffrey L. Bickersteth

On The Promontory

Lady, whose shrine stands on the promontory,
Pray for all those who are in ships, those
Whose business has to do with fish, and
Those concerned with every lawful traffic
And those who conduct them.

Repeat a prayer also on behalf of
Women who have seen their sons or husbands
Setting forth, and not returning:
Figlia del tuo figlio,
Queen of Heaven.

Also pray for those who were in ships, and
Ended their voyage on the sand, in the sea's lips
Or in the dark throat which will not reject them
Or wherever cannot reach them the sound of the sea bells'
Perpetual angelus.

T. S. ELIOT (1888–1965)

The Tear

What bright soft thing is this,
   Sweet Mary, thy fair eyes' expense?
A moist spark it is,
   A watery diamond, from whence
The very term, I think, was found,
The water of a diamond.

O, 'tis not a tear,
   'Tis a star about to drop
From thine eye, its sphere.
   The sun will stoop and take it up.
Proud will his sister be to wear
This thine eye's jewel in her ear.

O, 'tis a tear,
   Too true a tear, for no sad eyne,
How sad soe'er,
   Rain so true a tear as thine:
Each drop, leaving a place so dear,
Weeps for itself, is its own tear.

Such a pearl as this is
   (Slipp'd from Aurora's dewy breast)
The rose-bud's sweet lip kisses,
   And such the rose itself, that's vex'd
With ungentle flames, does shed,
Sweating in a too warm bed.

Such the maiden gem,
    By the purpling vine put on,
Peeps from her parent stem
    And blushes on the bridegroom sun:
The wat'ry blossom of thy eyne,
Ripe, will make the richer wine.

Fair drop, why quak'st thou so?
    'Cause thou straight must lay thy head
In the dust? O no,
    The dust shall never be thy bed:
A pillow for thee will I bring,
Stuff'd with down of angel's wing.

Thus carri'd up on high
    (For to Heaven thou must go),
Sweetly shalt thou lie
    And in soft slumbers bathe thy woe
Till the singing orbs awake thee
And one of their bright chorus make thee.

There thyself shalt be
    An eye, but not a weeping one;
Yet I doubt of thee
    Whether th' hadst rather there have shone
An eye of Heav'n, or still shine here
In the Heav'n of Mary's eye, a tear.

RICHARD CRASHAW (1613–1649)

The May Magnificat

May is Mary's month, and I
Muse at that and wonder why:
 Her feasts follow reason,
 Dated due to season —

Candlemas, Lady Day;
But the Lady Month, May,
 Why fasten that upon her,
 With a feasting in her honour?

Is it only its being brighter
Than the most are must delight her?
 Is it opportunest
 And flowers finds soonest?

Ask of her, the mighty mother:
Her reply puts this other
 Question: What is Spring? —
 Growth in every thing —

Flesh and fleece, fur and feather,
Grass and greenworld all together;
 Star-eyed strawberry-breasted
 Throstle above her nested

Cluster of bugle blue eggs thin
Forms and warms the life within;
 And bird and blossom swell
 In sod or sheath or shell.

The Madonna in the Rose Garden. *Stefano da Verona*

All things rising, all things sizing
Mary sees, sympathising
 With that world of good,
 Nature's motherhood.

Their magnifying of each its kind
With delight calls to mind
 How she did in her stored
 Magnify the Lord.

Well but there was more than this:
Spring's universal bliss
 Much, had much to say
 To offering Mary May.

When drop⁄of⁄blood⁄and⁄foam⁄dapple
Bloom lights the orchard⁄apple
 And thicket and thorp are merry
 With solver⁄surfed cherry.

And azuring⁄over greyball makes
Wood banks and brakes wash wet like lakes
 And magic cuckoocall
 Caps, clears, and clinches all –

This ecstasy all through mothering earth
Tells Mary her mirth till Christ's birth
 To remember and exultation
 In God who was her salvation.

GERARD MANLEY HOPKINS (1844–1889)

Our Lady of Walsingham

There once the penitents took off their shoes
And then walked barefoot the remaining mile;
And the small trees, a stream and hedgerows file
Slowly along the munching English lane,
Like cows to the old shrine, until you lose
Track of your dragging pain.

The stream flows down under the druid tree,
Shiloah's whirlpools gurgle and make glad
The castle of God. Sailor, you were glad
And whistled Sion by that stream. But see:

Our Lady, too small for her canopy,
Sits near the altar. There's no comeliness
At all or charm in that expressionless
Face with its heavy eyelids. As before,
This face, for centuries a memory,
Non est species, neque decor,
Expressionless, expresses God: it goes
Past castled Sion. She knows what God knows,
Not Calvary's Cross nor crib at Bethlehem
Now, and the world shall come to Walsingham.

ROBERT LOWELL (1917–1977)

The Virgin. *From a fifteenth-century MS*

O Mooder Mayde!

From: The Prologue To The Prioress's Tale

O mooder Mayde! O mayde Mooder free!
O bussh unbrent, brennynge in Moyses' sighte,
That ravyshedest doun fro the Deitee,
Thurgh thyn humblesse, the Goost that in th' alighte
Of whos vertu, whan he thyn herte lighte,
Conceyved was the Fadre's sapience,
Help me to telle it in thy reverence.

Lady, thy bountee, thy magnificence,
Thy vertu, and thy grete humylitee,
Ther may no tonge expresse in no science;
For somtyme, Lady, er men praye to thee,
Thou goost biforn of thy benignytee
And getest us the lyght thurgh thy preyere
To gyden us unto thy Sone so deere.

GEOFFREY CHAUCER (?1343–1400)

John Beseeches Her

Don't lower the wave of my heart,
it swells to your eyes, Mother;
don't alter love, but bring the wave to me
in your translucent hands.

He asked for this.

I am John the fisherman. There isn't much
in me to love.

I feel I am still on that lake shore,
gravel crunching under my feet –
and, suddenly – Him.

You will embrace His mystery in me no more,
yet quietly I spread round your thoughts like myrtle.
And calling you Mother – His wish –
I beseech you: may this word
never grow less for you.

True, it's not easy to measure the meaning
of the words He breathed into us both
so that all earlier love in those words
should be concealed.

KAROL WOJTYLA (1920–   )
   (*Translated by Jerzy Peterkiewicz*)

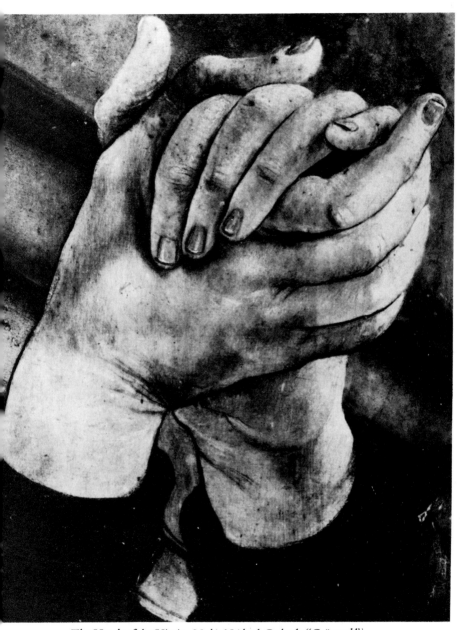

The Hands of the Virgin. *Mathis Neithard-Gothardt ('Grünewald')*

From: Sancta Maria Dolorosa or, The Mother of Sorrows: A Pathetical Descant upon the Devout Plainsong of Stabat Mater Dolorosa

In shade of death's sad tree
    Stood doleful she.
    Ah she! Now by none other
Name to be known, alas, but sorrow's mother.
    Before her eyes
    Hers and the whole world's joys
Hanging all torn she sees, and, in His woes
    And pains, her pangs and throes:
    Each wound of his, from every part,
    All more at home in her one heart.

    What kind of marble than
    Is that cold man
    Who can look on and see
Nor keep such noble sorrows company?
    Sure even from you,
    My flints, some drops are due,
To see so many unkind swords contest
    So fast for one soft breast
    While, with a faithful mutual flood,
    Her eyes bleed tears, his wounds weep blood.

The Virgin Mary. *Fourteenth-century stained glass*

O costly intercourse
Of deaths, and, worse,
Divided loves. While Son and mother
Discourse alternate wounds to one another,
Quick deaths that grow
And gather as they come and go,
His nails write swords in her, which soon her heart
Pays back with more than their own smart:
Her swords, still growing with his pain,
Turn spears and straight come home again.

She sees her Son, her God,
Bow with a load
Of borrow'd sins, and swim
In woes that were not made for him.
Ah! hard command
Of love! Here must she stand,
Charged to look on, and with a steadfast eye
See her life die,
Leaving her only so much breath
As serves to keep alive her death.

O mother turtle-dove!
Soft source of love!
That these dry lids might borrow
Something from thy full seas of sorrow!
O in that breast
Of thine (the noblest nest
Both of love's fires and floods) might I recline
This hard, cold heart of mine!
The chill lump would relent and prove
Soft subject for the siege of love.

O teach those wounds to bleed
In me, me, so to read
This book of loves, thus writ
In lines of death, my life may copy it
With loyal cares.
O let me, here, claim shares!
Yield something in thy sad prerogative,
Great queen of griefs, and give
Me too my tears; who, though all stone
Think much that thou should'st mourn alone.

The Virgin, Child and Cherubim. *Andrea Mantegna*

Rich queen, lend some relief,
  At least an alms of grief
To a heart who by sad right of sin
Could prove the whole sum (too sure) due to him.
      By all those stings
    Of love, bitter-sweet things,
Which these torn hands transcrib'd on thy true heart,
    O teach mine, too, the art
  To study him so till we mix
  Wounds and become one crucifix.

  Oh, let me suck the wine
    So long of this chaste vine
Till, drunk of the dear wounds, I be
A lost thing to the world, as it to me.
      O faithful friend
    Of me and of my end!
Fold up my life in love, and lay't beneath
    My dear Lord's vital death.
Lo, heart, thy hope's whole plea! her precious breath
Pour'd out in prayers for thee; thy Lord's in death.

RICHARD CRASHAW (1613–1649)

Our Lady of the Snow: Mount Righi

From: 'Memorials of a Tour, in 1820, on the Continent.'

Meek Virgin-Mother, more benign
Than fairest star, upon the height
Of thy own mountain, set to keep
Lone vigils through the hours of sleep,
What eye can look upon thy shrine
Untroubled at the sight?

These crowded offerings, as they hang
In sign of misery relieved,
Even these without intent of theirs,
Report of comfortless despairs,
Of many a deep and cureless pang
And confidence deceived.

To thee in this aërial cleft
As to a common centre, tend
All sufferers that no more rely
On mortal succour—all who sigh
And pine, of human hope bereft,
Nor wish for earthly friend.

And hence, O Virgin-Mother mild,
Though plenteous flowers around thee blow,
Not only from the dreary strife
Of winter, but the storms of life,
Thee have thy votaries aptly styled,
'Our Lady of the Snow.'

Even for the man who stops not here,
But down the irriguous valley hies,
Thy very name, O Lady, flings
O'er blooming fields and gushing springs
A tender sense of shadowy fear,
And chastening sympathies.

Nor falls that intermingling shade
To summer-gladsomeness unkind:
It chastens only to requite
With gleams of fresher, purer light;
While o'er the flower-enamelled glade
More sweetly breathes the wind.

But on — a tempting downward way,
A verdant path before us lies;
Clear shines the glorious sun above;
Then give free course to joy and love,
Deeming the evil of the day
Sufficient for the wise.

WILLIAM WORDSWORTH (1770–1850)

The Virgin and Angels. *From a ninth-century mosaic*

Pietà

Always the same hills
Crowd the horizon,
Remote witnesses
Of the still scene.

And in the foreground
The tall Cross,
Sombre, untenanted,
Aches for the Body
That is back in the cradle
Of a maid's arms.

R. S. THOMAS (1913–   )

The Virgin and Child. *Sandro Botticelli*

Life of the Virgin. *Bernardo Daddi*

III

Head of the Virgin. *Leonardo da Vinci*

On the Glorious Assumption of Our Blessed Lady

Hark! She is call'd. The parting hour is come.
Take thy farewell, poor world! Heav'n must go home
A piece of heav'nly earth, purer and brighter
Than the chaste stars, whose choice lamps come to light her
While through the crystal orbs, clearer than they,
She climbs and makes a far more milky way.
She's called. Hark how the dear immortal dove
Sighs to his silver mate, 'Rise up, my love!
'Rise up, my fair, my spotless one!
'The winter's past, the rain is gone.

'The spring is come, the flowers appear.
'No sweets but thou are wanting here.
   'Come away, my love!
   'Come away, my dove! Cast off delay.
   'The court of Heav'n is come
      'To wait upon thee home. Come, come away!
   'The flowers appear,
'Our quickly would, wert thou once here.
'The spring is come, or, if it stay,
''Tis to keep time with thy delay.
'The rain is gone, except so much as we
'Detain in needful tears to weep the want of thee.
      'The winter's past.
      'Or, if he make less haste,
'His answer is, Why, she does so.
'If summer come not, how can winter go?

Head of the Virgin. *Mainardi (Sebastiano di Bartolo)*

On the golden wings
Of the bright youth of Heav'n, that sings
Under so sweet a burthen. Go,
Since thy dread son will have it so.
And while thou goest our song and we
Will, as we may, reach after thee.
Hail, holy queen of humble hearts!
We in thy praise will have our parts.
    Thy precious name shall be
    Thy self to us, and we
    With holy care will keep it by us.
    We to the last
    Will hold it fast
    And no Assumption shall deny us.
    All the sweetest showers
    Of our fairest flowers
    Will we strow upon it.
    Though our sweets cannot make
    It sweeter, they can take
    Themselves new sweetness from it.

The Madonna of the Girdle. *Matteo di Giovanni*

'Maria', men and angels sing,
'Maria, mother of our King.'
   Live, rosy princess, live. And may the bright
Crown of a most incomparable light
Embrace thy radiant brows. O may the best
Of everlasting joys bath thy white breast.
Live, our chaste love, the holy mirth
Of Heav'n, the humble pride of earth.
Live, crown of women, queen of men.
Live mistress of our song. And when
Our weak desires have done their best,
Sweet angels, come and sing the rest.

RICHARD CRASHAW (1613–1649)

Notre Dame. *Georges Rouault*

The Madonna and Child. *From a ninth-century mosaic*

Mary, Be our Succour and Help

Marye, goddis modir dere,
Socoure & helpe us while we ben here,
   Gouerne, wisse and rede.
As thou art modir, mayden and wijf,
Clense us fro synne and graunte good lijf,
   And helpe us in oure nede.

ANONYMOUS

The Death of the Virgin. *Fifteenth-century woodcut*

Index of Poets

Index of Artists

SVPER OVNCTAS BENEDIC
LA QVE ST OHSVE ROSCIS